漢光家常菜系列(二)

珍饈小館

Highlight's Chinese Gourmet Cooking

豬牛類 Pork & Beef Dishes

序

漢光從事食譜製作已逾十年。十年來，我們出版了近三十種不同的食譜，有一般家常菜也有知名地方菜；有育兒類也有保健類，最近流行的微波爐食譜亦羅列其中。這些食譜主題雖異，卻都是爲了增進人類更美善的生活而編，並期許做一個中華飲食文化的傳薪者。

「珍饈小館」是考慮現代上班族的需要，新編的一套小食譜。全套分六册，係依材料區分（豬牛肉類、雞鴨肉類、海鮮類、蔬菜類、滋補類、點心類），每册再循烹調法排序（炒、炸、煎、燒、蒸、烤、醃、拌、煮〔湯〕)，只有第五册因目的不同，改以三餐排序。如果您學會了炒肉，即可利用同法炒雞丁、魚片；因此，當您在編排菜單時，就懂得把煎、炒菜式搭配著蒸、煮菜式上桌。不僅調和色香味，也可節省做菜時間，例如：先做蒸菜，再做炒的菜，實在是一種極科學的方法。

這套小食譜仍採中、英對照，是爲了方便海外讀者也可以按照這簡明的步驟，和中國人一齊享受自己動手做菜的樂趣。

漢光文化事業股份有限公司　總經理

宋定西

FOREWORD

Hilit has been working on Chinese recipes production for more than ten years. In the past decade, it has published up to 30 kinds of recipes, including those of homemade, regional, diet, tonic, and microwave dishes. These are Hilit's renowned records on introducing genuine Chinese food in a modern-oriented design.

In this new entry, Highlight Chinese Cuisine (II), the focus has been laid on fulfilling the need of the hustled nine-to-five workers. The series has 6 volumns, divided by ingredient and usage, which namely include, beef and pork, chicken and duck, seafood, vegetarian, tonic, and dimsum dishes. In each volumn, the dishes are grouped according to cooking methods (stir-frying, deep-frying, shallow-frying, stewing, steaming, baking, pickling, cold-mixing, and boiling [soup].) It will be convenient for the reader to compile his own recipes and plan cooking steps in various occasions.

目錄
CONTENTS

一、如何分辨優質肉品：

● **豬肉**

質好的肉，瘦肉部分是呈淡紅色，有光澤，脂肪呈白色油光發亮，用手撫觸，感覺肉堅實而有彈性；質差的肉，表面有一層風乾的硬皮，色澤暗淡，呈白色或灰色，肉質軟而無彈性；變質的肉，有黏性，分泌物流出，色澤青藍。另外，毛皮細小的，多爲嫩豬，毛孔粗糙的，多爲老豬。

● **牛肉**

質好的肉,呈鮮紅色（如是老牛肉,則呈紫紅色）,肉質結實而有光澤，肌肉的纖維較細，如以手指按，有彈性感覺；質差的，與上述的現象相反，無光澤，肉質鬆軟，纖維較粗，以手指按，肉凹處不能立即復原。牛肉和羊肉的變質是由外到內；豬肉的變質，則是從內到外。

二、肉品分部食用法：

● **豬肉**

①豬頭肉　包括嘴、耳、頭肉。適合作滷菜、開胃食品。

②前腿肉　包括髼頭、不見天。前腿肉適合做叉燒；不見天部位適合燒；靠近脊部的髼頭，可以絞碎，也可炒做豬排或咕嚕肉。

③後腿　包括柳肉。肉厚嫩、瘦肉多，適合拉絲、炒或做豬排等；柳肉肉質細滑，色稍深紅，適合於炒。

④里脊肉　是豬肉中之精品，一隻豬中祇有兩條。肉紋細，川湯、炒都很適合。

⑤肥肉頭　近肉眼處，肉肥爽，適合做肉卷。

⑥花肉　包括排骨部位。肥瘦間層，稱爲五花肉，適合紅燒，不適於炸；排骨適合蒸、燒、炸或做糖醋排骨。

⑦泡腩　是豬肉中的次品，韌而肥，味道亦較差，多用於燉熟後切片。

⑧豬肘　就是斬去豬手、腳後的兩節肘肉，適合紅燒或燉。

⑨豬手、腳　適合紅燒或燉。

⑩豬尾　用途不廣，多半用來燒、燉。

● **牛肉**

①頸肉　質較劣，可用於紅燒、煨湯、製餡。

②上腦　位於脊背前部，靠近後腦，帶有肥肉而嫩，適合烤、炒。

③前腿　位於上腦下部位置，包括前腦腱子上部。肉質較軟，適合烤、炒、爆等；里脊肉質細而嫩，用於爆、炒等。

④腰窩頭　位於背脊部，下連牛柳。肉質厚潤而肥嫩，適合炒及燒。
⑤柳肉　有兩條，是全隻牛中最嫩的部位。肉紋細而滑，肉味香而鮮，切片、拉絲皆宜，適合炒和製作較好的菜肴。
⑥胸腩　位於腹部。呈帶狀，肉層較薄，有白筋的適合紅燒；柔軟部份適合爆、炒等。
⑦米龍　位於尾根部，前部緊接牛排。肉嫩、表上有脂肪，適於炸、溜、爆、炒等。
⑧後腿　肉質較幼嫩，適合炒或做剁肉之用。
⑨前腱子　肉質很堅硬，適合紅燒、滷、醬等。
⑩後腱子　肉質較硬，用於滷、醬、紅燒等。
⑪牛尾　肥肉較多，適合煨湯。

HOW TO CHOOSE QUALITY PORK AND BEEF

- **Pork**

The meat should be pinkish-gray and have white, lustrous fat. It should feel firm and slightly springy in hands. The younger pork has a softer skin. The deteriorating process of pork is inside out, so check the color and texture closely when choose.

- **Beef**

The meat should be red or scarlet (the older beef has a darker color); feel firm and slightly springy and have a luster. The texture should be smooth and delicate. The deteriorating process of beef is outside in.

COOKING DIFFERENT PARTS OF PORK

1. Head and Facial meat: Can be used to make *lu* dishes or appetizers.
2. Shoulder: Includes Boston shoulder and picnic shoulder. It can be used to make Char Siu. The picnic shoulder is used braised or fried; the Boston shoulder can be sliced into steaks or used ground, diced in frying dishes.
3. Leg: Includes the sirloin end. It is tender and meaty; can be cut into slices and roasted, fried, and broiled. The sirloin end has a delicate texture; it is usually used in frying dishes.
4. Double Loin Roast: Finest part of pork. It has two strings; can be

broiled or fried.

5. Center Loin: The meat is thick and tender; can be used to make meat roll.
6. Bacon and Spareribs: Bacon can be red-cooked, not good for frying. Spareribs can be steamed, braised, or fried; especially tasty for Sweet and Sour dishes.
7. Belly: Contains more fat and is chewy after cooked. Usually considered sub-class part of pork, while it can be delicious if properly simmered.
8. Hock, 9. Feet, 10. Tail: Can be red-cooked or simmered.

COOKING DIFFERENT PARTS OF BEEF

1. Neck: Sub-class part of beef; can be red-cooked, broiled, or used for ground meat.
2. Blade: Tender and has fat; can be fried or roasted.
3. Shoulder: Includes chuck and the upper part of brisket. The meat is tender and can be roasted and fried.
4. Top Loin: Thick and tender, can be sliced then fried or stewed.
5. Center Loin: Includes the front part of sirloin. Finest part of beef; the texture is tender and delicate. Can be sliced or shredded then used in frying dishes, or banquet dishes.
6. Belly: Thin meat with white gluten; the gluten part can be red-cooked and the tender meat used in frying and crackling dishes.
7. Rump: Tender, with fat; can be stir-fried, crackling-fried, and deep-fried.
8. Bottom Round: Tender and delicate; can be fried and often chopped before used.
9. Fore Shank, 10. Hind Shank: Hard; can be red-cooked, *lu*, or curred.
11. Tail: Has much fat; can be broiled.

魚香茄子

FISH-FRAGRANT EGGPLANT

主要營養成份Major Nutrient Content：

蛋白質 Protein	脂肪 Fat	醣類 Carbohydrate	鈉 Sodium	膽固醇 Cholesterol	總熱量 Total
20.5 g	100 g	21 g	1500mg	——	1066Cal

材料：

茄子450公克、太白粉1小匙、麻油1小匙、胡椒¼小匙、油½杯。

①絞肉120公克、蒜末2小匙、薑末2小匙、葱（切花）1根、辣豆瓣醬1小匙。

調味料：

鹽¼小匙、糖½小匙、醋¼小匙、酒1小匙、醬油1大匙、高湯（或水）¼杯。

做法：

1.茄子洗淨，切成5公分長段；混合①料；混合調味料，備用。

2.油入鍋燒熱，放入茄子，翻炒至軟（約5分鐘），盛起備用。

3.鍋中留下1湯匙油加熱，放入①料翻炒至豬肉變色，再入調味料及茄子，待滾後轉至中火，蓋上鍋蓋燜1分鐘。用太白粉加水勾芡，加上麻油及胡椒後即可食。

建議：

此道菜主要熱量來自魚香肉末和大量的油，因此所用的絞肉切忌用三層肉，否則會使含油量更高。

Ingredients

450g eggplant, 1 teaspoon cornstarch, 1 teaspoon sesame oil, ¼ teaspoon ground Sichuan pepper, ½ cup oil.

Meat Mixture

120g ground pork, 2 teaspoons finely chopped garlic, 2 teaspoons finely chopped ginger, 1 chopped whole scallion, 1 teaspoon hot bean sauce.

Seasoning

¼ teaspoon salt, ½ teaspoon sugar, ¼ teaspoon vinegar, 1 teaspoon wine, 1 tablespoon soy sauce, ¼ cup broth or water.

Method

1. Peel eggplant if the skin is tough. Cut lengthwise into finger-size strips. Assemble Meat Mixture and Seasoning.
2. Heat oil until hot, add eggplant. Turn heat to medium and stir intermittently until soft (about 5 minutes). Push to side of work to press out excess oil with a spatula. Set eggplant aside.
3. Pour out all but 1 tablespoon oil. Heat until hot. Stir Meat Mixture until pork changes color. Add Seasoning and eggplant. When it boils, turn heat to medium, cover, and simmer for 1 minute. Thicken with cornstarch mixed with some water. Add sesame oil and Sichuan pepper.

蠔油雪豆牛肉

BEEF AND SNOWPEAS IN OYSTER SAUCE

主要營養成份 Major Nutrient Content：

蛋白質 Protein	脂肪 Fat	醣類 Carbohydrate	鈉 Sodium	膽固醇 Cholesterol	總熱量 Total
60 g	59 g	24 g	2030mg	——	867Cal

材料：

牛里脊肉300公克、洋葱1小個、豌豆2杯、油3大匙、水2大匙。

醃料：

太白粉1小匙、醬油1小匙、酒1小匙、蠔油醬1大匙。

調味料：

鹽少許、醬油1大匙。

做法：

1.將牛肉切成片，以醃料浸置15分鐘；豌豆洗淨；洋葱切片。

2.鍋燒熱後，加入1湯匙油燒熱，洋葱入鍋翻炒，火轉小，加入豌豆翻炒，再加鹽，即先盛起備用。

3.鍋燒熱，放入2湯匙油燒熱。牛肉入鍋，快速炒至將熟，加入洋葱、豌豆、水和醬油，再翻炒幾下即可上桌。

備註：

可以青椒或蘆筍代替豌豆。

建議：

蠔油醬亦含有高量的鈉，不宜用太多。

Ingredients

300g beef (sirloin or flank), 1 small onion, 2 cups snowpeas, 3 tablespoons oil, 2 tablespoons water.

Marinade

1 teaspoon cornstarch, 1 teaspoon soy sauce, 1 teaspoon wine, 1 tablespoon oyster sauce.

Seasoning

Pinch of salt, 1 tablespoon soy sauce.

Method

1. Cut beef across the grain into 0.4cm slices. Combine with Marinade and let stand for 15 minutes.
2. Chop onion coarsely. String snowpeas and rinse. Heat wok over high flame until smoking. Add one tablespoon oil, which should be heated in seconds. Stir onion briefly (turn heat lower if it tends to burn). Add snowpeas and stir briefly. Sprinkle salt while stirring. Set aside.
3. Heat wok again over high flame until smoking. Heat the remaining 2 tablespoons oil in the wok until very hot. Stir beef in quickly, until it is almost cooked. Add onion, snowpeas, water and soy sauce. Stir a few times and serve.

Other Applications

Substitute other vegetables, such as green peppers and asparagus, for snowpeas.

京醬肉絲

PORK SHREDS IN PEKING SAUCE

主要營養成份 Major Nutrient Content：

蛋白質 Protein	脂肪 Fat	醣類 Carbohydrate	鈉 Sodium	膽固醇 Cholesterol	總熱量 Total
59 g	161 g	66 g	1000mg	297mg	1949Cal

材料：

瘦豬肉350公克、葱絲（10公分長）2杯、油¼杯。

醃料：

太白粉1小匙、醬油1大匙、酒1大匙、水1大匙。

調味料：

海鮮醬2大匙、麻油½小匙。

做法：

1.瘦肉切絲，加入醃料拌勻，放置15分鐘。

2.油入鍋燒熱，加入肉絲，炒至熟，移至碗中。

3.鍋中留油，燒熱後轉中火，加入海鮮醬，翻炒數下，再加入肉絲炒20秒鐘。濾去鍋中油，灑下麻油，拌勻。盛入預先排好葱絲的盤子。

備註：

依此法可做京醬牛肉絲。

Ingredients

350g lean pork, 2 cups shredded scallions, ¼ cup oil.

Marinade

1 teaspoon cornstarch, 1 tablespoon dark soy sauce, 1 tablespoon wine, 1 tablespoon water.

Seasoning

2 tablespoons hoisin sauce, ½ teaspoon sesame oil.

Method

1. Cut pork into 0.4cm shreds. Add Marinade and stir until liquid is absorbed. Let stand for 15 minutes. Line bottom of serving platter with scallions.
2. Heat ¼ cup oil in wok until hot, fry pork until color turns pale. Remove pork with slotted spoon. Leave oil in wok.
3. Heat oil again until hot. Turn heat to medium. Fry hoisin sauce briefly. Add meat and stir for 20 seconds. Pour off excess oil. Sprinkle with sesame oil and pour over scallions. Mix the two at the table.

Other Applications

Beef Shreds in Peking Sauce: Substitute beef for pork.

葱爆羊肉

SCALLIONED LAMB

主要營養成份 Major Nutrient Content：

蛋白質 Protein	脂肪 Fat	醣類 Carbohydrate	鈉 Sodium	膽固醇 Cholesterol	總熱量 Total
78 g	104 g	9 g	2000mg	337mg	1284Cal

材料：

羊肉350公克、油3大匙、蒜末1大匙、芫荽（切好）1棵。

①蔥（連葉切絲）2杯、醬油1大匙、麻油1大匙。

醃料：

太白粉1小匙、辣椒粉1小匙、醬油1大匙、油1小匙。

做法：

1.羊肉切成薄片，與醃料拌合醃置15分鐘。

2.油入鍋燒熱，蒜入鍋，爆香，加入羊肉絲翻炒至變色，加入①料，炒30秒鐘，灑上芫荽，盛起，趁熱吃。

備註：

依此法可做葱爆牛肉。以牛腰肉代替羊肉，唯辣椒粉應減少，因爲牛肉味道不比羊肉強烈。蒜和麻油量亦可減少，甚至省略。

Ingredients

350g lamb, 3 tablespoons oil, 1 tablespoon finely sliced garlic, 1 chopped stalk fresh coriander.

Marinade

1 teaspoon cornstarch, 1 teaspoon ground Sichuan pepper, 1 tablespoon soy sauce, 1 teaspoon oil.

Seasoning

2 cups shredded scallions, 1 tablespoon soy sauce, 1 tablespoon sesame oil.

Method

1. Slice lamb into as thin slices as possible. Combine with Marinade. Let stand for 15 minutes. Combine Seasoning.
2. Heat oil until very hot. Fry garlic until aromatic. Add lamb and stir quickly until color changes. Add Seasoning. Stir for 30 seconds. Garnish with coriander and serve immediately.

Other Applications

Scallioned Beef: Substitute flank steak for lamb. Substitute a pinch of ground pepper for Sichuan pepper. Since beef is not as strong-tasting as lamb, you would want to use less garlic and sesame oil, or even omit both.

八寶辣醬

SPICED EIGHT-JEWELS

主要營養成份 Major Nutrient Content：

蛋白質 Protein	脂肪 Fat	醣類 Carbohydrate	鈉 Sodium	膽固醇 Cholesterol	總熱量 Total
68 g	226 g	66 g	2450mg	150mg	2525Cal

材料：

豬五花肉200公克、蝦米37.5公克、豆干16塊、花生仁½飯碗、小玉米筍5支、筍200公克、菱角肉12顆、青豌豆20公克、葱1根、薑2片、油5大匙。

調味料：

辣椒醬3大匙、醬油½大匙、酒2大匙、鹽1小匙、砂糖2小匙。

做法：

1.豬肉洗淨，帶皮切成小丁；豆干洗淨，切成小丁；蝦米去殼略洗，加1大匙酒、1大匙水醃浸；玉米筍洗淨，切成小丁；筍去籜，週圍削淨，切成小丁；葱去根切小段；菱肉略洗，對切為二；豌豆略沖洗；花生仁用熱水泡，將衣剝除。

2.豬肉入鍋中，加水和葱、薑、酒煮至半熟時盛起。湯汁留在鍋中，菱肉、筍丁、花生和入，續煮數沸，豌豆落鍋又煮兩沸起鍋。

3.鍋中入油，將葱段爆香，辣醬倒下，炒至醬香四溢時盛起。

4.鍋中又入油煮沸，先炒蝦米，隨即將豆干傾下煸炒，至微黃色時起鍋，再入肉丁稍加醬油和水，煮至肉將酥時，薑片挾出。豆干、筍丁、菱角、花生、豌豆等一併倒下，醬和入，酌加砂糖炒勻，加少許水煮兩沸，隨時翻炒，以免粘鍋，待湯汁收少後盛起，即可供食。

建議：

油脂含量較高，高血壓者不宜食用。

Ingredients

200g belly of pork, 3 squares beancurd, 50g canned baby corn, 200g bamboo shoots, 50g water chestnuts, 25g peanuts, 50g cooked prawns, 25g peas, 2 spring onions, 4 slices ginger, 5 tablespoons oil.

Seasoning

2 tablespoon rice wine, 2 tablespoons chilli-bean sauce, 2 teaspoons soy sauce, 2 teaspoons sugar, 1 teaspoon salt and pepper.

Method

1. Cut pork into 2cm slices. Cut beancurd into 2cm cubes. Dice baby corn and bamboo shoots. Skin peanuts and deep-fry in moderately hot oil until golden. Drain. Cut 1 spring onion into sections.
2. Put pork slices into a pan with 2 slices ginger, 1 whole spring onion, the rice wine and 500ml water. Simmer for 20 minutes, then lift out and reserve stock.
3. Heat 3 tablespoons oil in a pan and stir-fry the remaining onion and ginger.
4. Add the pork, then the vegetables and prawns. Pour in the reserved stock, chilli-bean sauce and soy sauce and bring to the boil. Slide in the beancurd and simmer for 5 minutes. Adjust the seasoning with salt, sugar and pepper and mix in the peanuts before serving.

糖醋波蘿排骨

SWEET AND SOUR PINEAPPLE SPARERIBS

主要營養成份 Major Nutrient Content：

蛋白質 Protein	脂肪 Fat	醣類 Carbohydrate	鈉 Sodium	膽固醇 Cholesterol	總熱量 Total
208 g	198 g	68 g	3000mg	——	2886Cal

材料：

小排骨1200公克、醬油2大匙、蒜2粒、青椒1個、番茄1個、鳳梨（罐頭）片½杯、油1大匙、炸油適量。

調味料：

水½杯、太白粉2大匙、醋3大匙、醬油1大匙、糖2大匙、鳳梨汁（罐頭）½杯。

做法：

1. 小排骨剁成5公分小段，放入開水中燒煮至沒有血水（可用筷子試），約20分鐘後撈起，瀝乾，再以醬油醃泡20分鐘，撈起置於盤中，晾乾約1小時。
2. 蒜拍碎；青椒去籽洗淨，切成3公分大小方塊；番茄切成小塊。混合調味料備用。
3. 將炸油燒至175°C，放入小排骨炸至金黃（約1分鐘），撈出瀝油，置於盤中。
4. 1湯匙油入鍋中燒熱，蒜放入爆香，再放入青椒翻炒，加入調味料翻炒至微稠，再放進番茄、鳳梨片炒勻，淋在排骨上即可，趁熱吃。

Ingredients

1200g small pork ribs, 2 tablespoons dark soy sauce, 2 cloves garlic, 1 green pepper, 1 tomato, ½ cup canned pineapple chunks, 1 tablespoon oil for stir-frying.

Sauce

½ cup water, 2 tablespoons cornstarch, 2 tablespoons sugar, 3 tablespoons vinegar, 1 tablespoon dark soy sauce, ½ cup juice from canned pineapple chunks.

Method

1. Ask the butcher to cut across the bones into three strips, then separate the ribs. Boil them in a large pot of boiling water until no more pink juice comes out when pierced with a fork, about 20 minutes. Drain and marinate with 2 tablespoons dark soy sauce for 20 minutes. Spread out on tray to dry, about 1 hour.
2. Smash and peel garlic. Cut pepper into 3cm squares. Cut tomato into chunks. Assemble Sauce ingredients.
3. Heat 1 tablespoon oil in saucepan. Add garlic and stir until aromatic. Stir in pepper. Add Sauce ingredients and stir until thickened. Add tomato and pineapple. Keep warm.
4. Have a skimmer on hand. Heat frying oil to 175°C. Fry ribs until brown, about 1 minute. Transfer to serving platter. Pour Sauce over ribs and serve hot.

拂手排骨

FEATHER-DUSTER SPARERIBS

主要營養成份 Major Nutrient Content：

蛋白質 Protein	脂肪 Fat	醣類 Carbohydrate	鈉 Sodium	膽固醇 Cholesterol	總熱量 Total
61 g	127 g	89 g	5200mg	352mg	920Cal

材料：

小排骨整支（長約5～9公分）12根、鳳梨¼個、胡蘿蔔¼根、洋葱½個、葱2根、油1大碗。

調味料：

太白粉3大匙、番茄醬2大匙、醬油、糖、醋、酒各2大匙。

做法：

1.小排骨洗淨後，每根由二分之一處刮去肉後置於碗中，加入1大匙的太白粉、醬油、醋、糖、酒，拌和，漬30分鐘。

2.鍋中入油煮沸，將排骨倒入，以小火邊炸邊翻動，待炸成黃色時撈起，濾去油汁排入盤中。

3.炸油倒出，鍋子清除後舀入2大匙油，煮至沸時，入蘿蔔丁、鳳梨丁、洋葱丁同炒，加1大匙醬油、糖、番茄醬及4大匙水煮沸，下太白粉水勾芡，澆淋在排骨上，即可供食。

建議：

醣類主要來自太白粉及糖，糖尿病者應注意之。

Ingredients

12 pork ribs (each 5-9cm long), 50g fresh or canned pineapple, 50g carrot, 50g onion, 2 spring onions, oil for deep frying.

Seasoning

2 tablespoons cornflour, 2 tablespoons soy sauce, 2 tablespoons rice wine, pinch of salt, 2 tablespoons rice vinegar, 2 tablespoons sugar, 1 tablespoon tomato paste.

Method

1. Marinate pork ribs with 1 tablespoon each of cornflour, soy sauce, rice wine and a dash of salt; let stand for ½ hour. Cube pineapple and carrot. Shred onion and dice spring onions. Make cornflour paste with the remaining cornflour.
2. Heat oil in a pan, then add the ribs. Deep-fry over a moderate heat until golden brown. Lift out, drain and place the ribs on a plate. Heat 2 tablespoons oil in a clean pan over a high flame. Stir-fry carrot, onion and pineapple. Add 1 tablespoon soy sauce, the vinegar, sugar, tomato paste and 4 tablespoons water; bring to the boil. Add cornflour paste to thicken. Pour over the ribs and serve.

煎豬排

PORK CUTLET IN HOISIN SAUCE

主要營養成份 Major Nutrient Content：

蛋白質 Protein	脂肪 Fat	醣類 Carbohydrate	鈉 Sodium	膽固醇 Cholesterol	總熱量 Total
67 g	142 g	24 g	3960mg	——	1642Cal

材料：

豬里脊肉（或2.5公分厚豬排）450公克、薑3片、葱（切花）2根、油2大匙。

醃料：

鹽½茶匙、胡椒粉¼小匙、太白粉1大匙、酒1小匙、醬油1大匙、麻油（可省略）1小匙。

調味料：

海鮮醬1大匙、醬油1大匙、番茄醬2大匙、高湯（或水）6大匙。

做法：

1.逆著里脊紋理切成1.5公分厚肉片後，浸於醃料中15分鐘。

2.炒鍋燒熱，肉片入鍋用中火煎至顏色改變，翻面亦同，先盛起備用。

3.油留鍋再燒熱，放入薑、葱炒30秒鐘，加入調味料與豬肉。蓋上鍋蓋，中火慢煮5分鐘，偶而翻動，最後揀去薑即可上桌。

Ingredients

450g tenderloin or 2.5cm thick pork chops, 3 slices ginger, 2 whole scallions (cut into 5cm sections), 2 tablespoons oil.

Marinade

½ teaspoon salt, ¼ teaspoon pepper, 1 tablespoon cornstarch, 1 teaspoon wine, 1 tablespoon light soy sauce, 1 teaspoon sesame oil (optional).

Sauce

1 tablespoon hoisin sauce, 1 tablespoon light soy sauce, 2 tablespoons ketchup, 6 tablespoons broth or water.

Method

1. Cut tenderloin across grain into 1.5cm slices. Combine with Marinade. Let stand for 15 minutes. Assemble Sauce.
2. Heat 2 tablespoons oil in frying pan. Over medium heat, fry pork until color changes. Turn and repeat. Set aside. Leave oil in pan.
3. Heat pan again and stir ginger and scallions for ½ minute. Add Sauce ingredients and pork. Cover and simmer over medium heat for 5 minutes. Turn occasionally. Discard ginger and serve hot. May be kept warm, refrigerated, or frozen and re-heated.

牛爬樹

CATTLE CLIMBING ON TREES

主要營養成份 Major Nutrient Content：

蛋白質 Protein	脂肪 Fat	醣類 Carbohydrate	鈉 Sodium	膽固醇 Cholesterol	總熱量 Total
92 g	54 g	27 g	2480mg	——	962Cal

材料：

牛里脊肉（或脊背肉）450公克、芥蘭菜225公克、油2大匙。

醃料：

蒜粉½小匙、胡椒粉¼小匙、五香粉少許、太白粉1小匙、醬油1大匙、酒1大匙。

調味料：

蠔油醬1大匙、番茄醬1大匙、醬油1大匙、水½小匙、太白粉2小匙。

做法：

1.牛肉逆紋切成約1.5公分厚的肉片，浸泡在醃料中1小時。

2.洗淨芥蘭菜，剝去梗上老皮，放入燒滾的開水中燙2分鐘，撈起入冷水中冷卻。冷卻後，將芥蘭同一方向平放盤中，切成三段。

3.油入鍋中燒熱，肉片平放鍋中，煎½～1分鐘，再煎熟另一邊，鏟起，平置芥蘭菜上。

4.將調味料與鍋中留油同炒，直至稠狀，淋在牛肉上即可。

Ingredients

450g sirloin or chunk, 225g Chinese broccoli, 2 tablespoons oil.

Marinade

½ teaspoon garlic powder, ¼ teaspoon pepper, a pinch of five-spice powder (optional), 1 teaspoon cornstarch, 1 tablespoon soy sauce, 1 tablespoon wine.

Sauce

½ cup water, 2 teaspoons cornstarch, 1 tablespoon oyster sauce, 1 tablespoon catchup, 1 tablespoon soy sauce.

Method

1. Slice beef against the grain into large, 1.5cm slices. Combine with Marinade and let stand for 1 hour. Assemble Sauce ingredients.
2. Wash broccoli and peel stems. Drop into a large pot of boiling water. Drain after two minutes. Rinse in cold water to cool. Squeeze out excess water. Arrange broccoli in one direction on platter; cut across twice.
3. Heat 2 tablespoons oil in frying pan or wok until hot. Fry beef, a single layer at a time, less than 1 minute on each side. Arrange pieces over broccoli.
4. Add Sauce ingredients to the oil left in the pan. Heat until thickens. Pour over beef and serve hot.

鑲豆腐

STUFFED BEAN CURD

主要營養成份 Major Nutrient Content：

蛋白質 Protein	脂肪 Fat	醣類 Carbohydrate	鈉 Sodium	膽固醇 Cholesterol	總熱量 Total
48 g	108 g	19 g	3000mg	——	1240Cal

材料：

豆腐450公克、蝦米1大匙、太白粉水1大匙、葱花少許、油2大匙、鹽½小匙。

①溫水1大匙、葱1根、荸薺4顆、豬肉(絞碎)110公克、薑汁¼小匙、麻油½小匙。

調味料：

高湯1杯、醬油2大匙。

做法：

1.豆腐切成7×7×2.5公分的立方塊，再斜切成三角形，沿著長邊用茶匙挖一裂口（留約0.7公分的邊）。

2.蝦米浸泡清水中10分鐘，撈起瀝乾（浸汁留用）。將蝦米、葱和荸薺一齊剁碎，所有①料均勻混合，填入豆腐裂口。

3.油放入平鍋中燒熱，轉中火，先將豆腐開口的一邊煎至金黃，然後再煎黃各面，加入高湯和醬油。待燒滾後，轉小火，慢煮3分鐘。

4.豆腐先盛至盤中，湯汁留在鍋中，加入太白粉水勾芡，將汁液淋上豆腐，再灑上葱花即可食。

Ingredients

450g firm bean curd, 2 tablespoons oil.

Stuffing

1 tablespoon dried shrimp, 1 tablespoon warm water, 1 whole scallion, 4 water chestnuts, 110g ground pork, ¼ teaspoon ginger juice, ½ teaspoon sesame oil (optional).

Seasoning

½ teaspoon salt, 1 cup broth (seasoned with salt), 2 tablespoons dark soy sauce, 1 teaspoon cornstarch, 1 whole scallion (chopped).

Method

1. Cut bean curd into squares, about 7×7×2.5cm. Cut each into 2 triangles. With a small knife, make a slit 0.7cm along the long side. Carve the center out. Scrape with a teaspoon.
2. Soak dried shrimp in warm water for 10 minutes. Drain and reserve liquid. Mince shrimp together with scallion and water chestnuts. Mix with the rest of Stuffing and reserved liquid. Use it to fill the pockets of bean curd.
3. Heat 2 tablespoons oil in frying pan, preferably the nonstick type. Over medium heat, stand the triangles with the opened side down in oil. Fry until light brown, while sprinkling with ½ teaspoon salt. Turn and brown the two broad sides also. Add broth and soy sauce. When it boils again, turn heat low and simmer for 3 minutes.
4. Transfer bean curd onto serving platter. Leave liquid in pan. Thicken with cornstarch mixed with some water. Pour over bean curd. Garnish with scallions.

碎肉餅

HAMBURGER PATTIES

主要營養成份 Major Nutrient Content：

蛋白質 Protein	脂肪 Fat	醣類 Carbohydrate	鈉 Sodium	膽固醇 Cholesterol	總熱量 Total
77 g	415 g	19 g	3915mg	420mg	4140Cal

材料：

絞肉600公克（豬肉牛肉均可）、洋葱½個、胡蘿蔔1小根、芹菜2～3根、沙拉油5大匙。

醃料：

黑胡椒粉¼小匙、醬油1大匙、鹽1小匙、糖1小匙、麻油2小匙、酒1小匙、薑汁2小匙（如用牛肉則尚可酌加¼小匙的蘇打粉或嫩精）。

淋料：

番茄醬適量。

做法：

1.絞肉（豬肉最好用夾心肉，¾是瘦肉¼是肥肉。或牛肉用全瘦的¾，另外¼用豬肥肉，不可用牛肥肉，因牛肉的肥肉味重，且涼後硬度較高故以豬肥肉較好。）加切碎的洋葱、胡蘿蔔及芹菜屑再加進所有調味料，用力而均勻地拌勻最好持續抓拌10分鐘使肉呈膠狀。

2.把拌好的肉做成一粒粒小圓餅形狀，（餅厚約1公分以內，直徑4～5公分）。一面做一面放進已加熱的放油的鍋中，以中火煎熟。煎的時間是每面2分鐘即可盛起，食時沾點番茄醬或甜辣醬均可，可做便當菜。

建議：

含鈉量較高，沾食用的番茄醬也含有鈉，高血壓患者需限量食用。

Ingredients

600g ground pork or ground beef, ½ small-sized onion, 1 small carrot, 2-3 celeries, 5 tablespoons corn oil, some catchup.

Dressing for Meat

¼ teaspoon black pepper, 1 tablespoon soy sauce, 1 teaspoon salt, 1 teaspoon sugar, 2 teaspoons sesame oil, 1 teaspoon sherry, 2 teaspoons ginger juice, ¼ teaspoon soda powder (If you use ground beef.)

Method

1. Mix crumbs of onion, carrot and celeries with ground pork (or ground beef) (About 80% lean). Add in seasoning and blend well. Use hand to blend for about 10 minutes.
2. Make the meat to patties. Grill the patties over medium heat in a pan with oil. Each patty should be less than half inch thick. Its diameter should be 4～5cm. Each side should be grilled for 2 minutes. Dip catchup of sweet and hot sauce to eat. The dish can be carried in lunch box.

Note

High sodium content for this dish. Hypertensives should restrain intake.

滷牛肉

LU BEEF

主要營養成份 Major Nutrient Content：

蛋白質 Protein	脂肪 Fat	醣類 Carbohydrate	鈉 Sodium	膽固醇 Cholesterol	總熱量 Total
169 g	57 g	30 g	8600mg	——	1309Cal

材料：

牛腱肉（或牛頸肉）900公克。

香料：

花椒1小匙、丁香8粒、桂皮1片、茴香1小匙、陳皮1片、乾辣椒2支、蒜2粒。

滷料：

醬油½杯、酒¼杯、水2杯、葱（切段）4根、薑4片、八角2粒、冰糖（或糖）2湯匙、麻油1小匙。

做法：

1. 香料包在小紗布袋中，連同牛肉、滷料放入鍋中同煮，待滾後，蓋上鍋蓋，轉小火，慢煮1小時（偶而翻動），加入冰糖後，再煮½小時。
2. 撈出牛肉，冷卻後再切片。濾出滷汁，取一部分與麻油混合，淋在肉片上，即可供食，冷食較佳。其餘滷汁可存於冰箱內，下次採用。

備註：

同法可滷豬肉、雞肉、鴨肉、豬肝、豬心、蛋等。也可多種材料同滷。

Ingredients

900g shank or chuck.

Sauce

½ cup dark soy sauce, ¼ cup wine, 2 cups water, 4 whole scallions, 4 thick slices ginger, 2 star anise.

Optional

1 teaspoon Sichuan peppercorn, 8 whole cloves, 1 Chinese cinnamon, 1 teaspoon fennel, 1 piece dried orange peel, 2 dried chili peppers, 2 cloves garlic.

---

2 tablespoons rock candy or sugar, 1 teaspoon sesame oil.

Method

1. Sew Optional ingredients of your choice, together with star anise, in a cloth bag. Place it with beef and Sauce ingredients in a heavy pot. Bring it to boil, cover and simmer over low heat for one hour. Turn occasionally. Add rock candy and continue simmering for another ½ hour.
2. Transfer the beef to a cutting board. Let cool. Slice it against the grain into large, thin slices. Strain the sauce. Use a portion of it and mix with sesame oil to sprinkle over the meat slices. Serve cold. Keep the excess *lu* in a jar for other *lu* dishes. It can be refrigerated for weeks or frozen indefinitely.

Other Applications

Use pork, chicken, duck, liver, heart, hard-boiled eggs, etc. to make various *lu* dishes. If you have already started the *lu*, you only need to add a portion of the above ingredients to the *lu* when you cook a new dish.

牛肉蓮藕

BEEF AND LOTUS ROOT SOUP

主要營養成份 Major Nutrient Content：

蛋白質 Protein	脂肪 Fat	醣類 Carbohydrate	鈉 Sodium	膽固醇 Cholesterol	總熱量 Total
90 g	26.5	36 g	2000mg	——	742.5Cal

材料：
蓮藕450公克、牛腱肉450公克、芫荽（切碎）1棵、醋少許、水6杯、鹽½小匙。
調味料：
醬油1大匙、酒2大匙、八角1粒、薑3片、葱1根。
做法：
1.蓮藕去皮，切成小塊；牛肉切成小塊。
2.水入鍋燒滾，加入所有調味料，再滾後，轉小火，慢煮至牛肉鬆軟（約2小時）。
3.揀去薑片和葱，放入鹽，再灑下芫荽屑和醋，即可供食，熱食佳。
備註：
依此法可做牛肉胡蘿蔔湯。牛肉先煮1½小時，再加入胡蘿蔔煮½小時。

Ingredients
450g lotus root, 450g shank or chuck, 6 cups water.
Seasoning
½ teaspoon salt, 1 tablespoon dark soy sauce, 2 tablespoons wine, 1 star anise, 3 slices ginger, 1 whole scallion.
Garnish
1 stalk fresh coriander or 1 whole scallion (chopped), a few drops of vinegar.
Method
1. Peel lotus root. Cube lotus root and beef.
2. Bring 6 cups water to boil. Add everything except Garnish. When it boils again, turn heat low, cover and simmer until tender, about 2 hours.
3. Discard ginger and scallion. Salt to taste. May be prepared ahead up to this point, refrigerated and reheated. Garnish and serve hot.

Other Applications
Beef and Carrot Soup: Substitute carrots for lotus root. Cook beef for 1½ hours. Add carrots. Cook for ½ hour more.

醬肉

BEAN SAUCE PORK

主要營養成份 Major Nutrient Content：

蛋白質 Protein	脂肪 Fat	醣類 Carbohydrate	鈉 Sodium	膽固醇 Cholesterol	總熱量 Total
132 g	284 g	39 g	5000mg	——	3240Cal

材料：

豬肉900公克、冰糖（或糖）2大匙、葱（切絲）1根、鹽½小匙。

醃料：

海鮮醬2大匙。

滷料：

醬油4大匙、酒1大匙、八角1粒、桂皮1片、薑3片、葱2棵、水¼杯。

做法：

1.豬肉整塊抹上鹽和海鮮醬，置於室溫中2小時，或置於冰箱一夜。

2.先在燉鍋中混合滷料，燒滾後，加入豬肉。再燒滾後，蓋上鍋蓋，轉小火慢煮1小時（需偶而攪動）加入冰糖後，繼續慢煮直至汁液變濃稠（但不要太乾）約½小時。

3.冷卻後，逆紋切成大薄片，排放盤中，倒入原煮肉濃汁，灑上葱絲，即可食，亦可於冰箱中冰置數天。

備註：

豬肉必須新鮮，帶些肥肉最好。

Ingredients

900g pork*.

Seasoning

4 tablespoons dark soy sauce, 1 tablespoon wine, 1 star anise, 1 piece Chinese cinnamon, 3 slices ginger, 2 whole scallions, ¼ cup water.

½ teaspoon salt, 2 tablespoons hoisin sauce, 2 tablespoons rock candy or sugar, fresh coriander (optional), 1 whole scallion (shredded).

* Use fresh meat with some fat, such as butt.

Method

1. Rub salt and hoisin sauce onto meat. Let stand for 2 hours, or overnight in the refrigerator.
2. In a heavy pot, bring Seasoning to boil. Add pork. When liquid boils again, cover, turn heat low and simmer for 1 hour. Turn occasionally. Add rock candy and continue Simmering until liquid is thick and reduced in volume, but not dry, about ½ hour. Let cool.
3. Slice against the grain into large, thin slice. Arrange on platter and pour liquid over. Garnish with scallion. Can be kept in refrigerator for several days or frozen indefinitely.

千張包

BEAN CURD ROLLS

主要營養成份 Major Nutrient Content：

蛋白質 Protein	脂肪 Fat	醣類 Carbohydrate	鈉 Sodium	膽固醇 Cholesterol	總熱量 Total
95 g	270 g	16 g	5605mg	303mg	2865Cal

材料：

五花絞肉375公克、荸薺4顆、蝦米乾1大匙、香菇數朵、高湯2碗、薑汁½大匙、沙拉油4大匙、百頁皮16張。

醃料：

紹興酒½大匙、胡椒粉¼小匙、鹽⅔小匙。

調味料：

鹽½小匙、醬油1大匙。

做法：

1. 荸薺拍碎；蝦米浸水1小時後取出剁碎；香菇泡清水2小時取出，去蒂切碎；全部加在絞肉中加醃料仔細拌勻。
2. 百頁皮一張舖開取約2大匙絞肉舖勻在其上，以一角對折起再折，然後左右二角向內折起，再包捲成5公分長段一枕形包。全部包好後排列在一小煮鍋內，再加進高湯、薑汁及調味料同以小火慢煮40分鐘，其間要上下翻動以免熟度不勻。
3. 如怕千張包散開可用麻繩把所有包好的千張包紮在一起再入鍋煮。
4. 食時如愛稀湯汁者可不必加太白粉勾芡，否則要淋少許芡汁，較為美觀。

建議：

百頁提供植物性蛋白質，是人體生長發育所必需。

Ingredients

375g ground pork (80% lean), 4 water chestnuts, 1 tablespoon dried baby shrimps, several dried black mushrooms, 2 cups stock, ½ tablespoon ginger juice, 4 tablespoons corn oil, 16 bean curd sheets.

Dressing for Meat

½ tablespoon sherry, ¼ teaspoon pepper, ⅔ teaspoon salt.

Seasoning

½ teaspoon salt, 1 tablespoon soy sauce.

Method

1. Crush water chestnuts. Soak dried baby shrimps in water for 1 hour. Chop dried baby shrimps into crumbs. Soak dried black mushrooms in water for 2 hours. Remove footstalks. Dice into crumbs. Blend all the crumbs with ground pork and dressing.
2. Wrap 2 tablespoons of the mix with one bean curd sheet. Fold one corner, then fold both the right and left corners. Roll into a 5cm long package. Array all the rolls in a pot. Add in soup stock, ginger juice and seasoning. Simmer over small heat for 40 minutes. Turn the rolls from side to side during simmering.
3. A hemp pope can be used to bind all the rolls together to avoid opening of the rolls.
4. Cornstarch water can be added to make the juice pasty if like.

竹節牛盅

BEEF IN BAMBOO BOWLS

主要營養成份 Major Nutrient Content：

蛋白質 Protein	脂肪 Fat	醣類 Carbohydrate	鈉 Sodium	膽固醇 Cholesterol	總熱量 Total
100 g	27 g	24 g	2500 g	——	739Cal

材料：

牛里脊肉450公克、干貝3粒、香菇6朵、荸薺6顆、高湯（可加入適量鹽）4杯、芫荽（切碎）1棵。

醃料：

溫水1杯、酒1湯匙。

調味料：

醬油2湯匙、鹽½小匙、胡椒粉⅛小匙。

做法：

1.里脊牛肉絞碎；干貝浸於醃料中一夜，撈起撕成細絲，浸汁留用。

2.香菇用溫水泡20分鐘，瀝乾去蒂，切成細絲；荸薺切片。

3.以上材料全部混合，慢慢加入高湯和留下的浸汁，並加攪動，再分裝入12個竹杯（或小碗）中，約¾滿。

4.鍋中燒開水，放上蒸籠，12小杯放進蒸籠。蓋上籠蓋，蒸15分鐘後，取出。每碗灑上芫荽，即可上桌。

Ingredients

450g sirloin, 3 dried scallops, 6 dried mushrooms, 1 cup water chestnuts, 4 cups broth (seasoned with salt), 1 cup warm water.

Seasoning

1 tablespoon wine, 2 tablespoons soy sauce, ½ teaspoon salt, ⅛ teaspoon ground pepper, 1 stalk fresh coriander.

Method

1. Have the butcher grind the beef twice. (You may grind the meat at home in a food processor). Soak dried scallops in 1 cup of warm water and 1 tablespoon wine overnight. Drain and reserve liquid. Chop scallops finely.
2. Soak mushrooms in warm water for 20 minutes. Discard liquid and stem. Chop fine. Chop water chestnuts coarsely.
3. Mix ingredients thoroughly. Gradually pour in broth and reserved liquid, stirring as you go. Place food in 12 bamboo cups or small bowls, about ¾ full.
4. Bring water in steamer to boil. Set bowls on steamer rack. Cover the steamer, and steam over high flame for 15 minutes. May be kept warm in the steamer briefly. Prolonged stay in the warm steamer tends to toughen the meat. Garnish each bowl with a sprig of coriander and serve hot.

富貴火腿

STEAMED SWEET HAM WITH BREAD

主要營養成份 Major Nutrient Content：

蛋白質 Protein	脂肪 Fat	醣類 Carbohydrate	鈉 Sodium	膽固醇 Cholesterol	總熱量 Total
142 g	296 g	359 g	6101mg	420mg	4663Cal

材料：

去皮火腿600公克（如帶皮的1500公克）、細蔴繩30公分、玻璃紙20公分四方1張、土司麵包1條。

調味料：

糖375公克。

做法：

1.火腿用溫水泡洗，刮去雜質和肉皮，刷洗清潔，切成3×2×0.5公分厚片，舖排在玻璃紙中央，糖150公克灑勻在火腿片上，包成長方形，用蔴繩綑縛，置於盤中。

2.鍋中入水煮沸，火腿置入，小火蒸約2小時（使火腿呈紅色而有黏性）。

3.將剩餘的糖倒入鍋中，微火熬成糖水。

4.火腿解包取出，去除蒸出之糖水，火腿排勻在長盤內，淋上熬好之糖水。

5.吐司去邊皮切成小片（一邊要相連），蒸（或烤）軟，裝在盤內一併上桌。

建議：

火腿爲醃漬品，含鈉量較高，高血壓者不宜食用，醣類幾乎皆由糖所來，所以糖尿病者不宜食用。

Ingredients

600g Chinese ham (boned, as a piece), 1 small white loaf.

Seasoning

380g crystal sugar.

Method

1. Soak the ham for 6 hours, then cut into slices 2×3cm and ½cm thick. Place in the bag and sprinkle 110g sugar over the ham. Tie into a tidy rectangular shape.
2. Steam the ham packet for about 2 hours over a low heat. It will turn red and slightly sticky.
3. Melt the remaining sugar in a pan to make a syrup.
4. Untie the packet and discard the gravy. Arrange the ham slices on a plate and pour over the syrup.
5. Trim the crust from the bread and slice so that every two slices are joined at one end, to make a V-shape. Steam until soft.

   Each person puts a slice of ham into a double slice of bread and holds it in their hand to eat.

珍珠肉圓

STEAMED PEARL BALLS

主要營養成份 Major Nutrient Content：

蛋白質 Protein	脂肪 Fat	醣類 Carbohydrate	鈉 Sodium	膽固醇 Cholesterol	總熱量 Total
70 g	143 g	64 g	3300mg	315mg	1850Cal

材料：

豬腿肉450公克、糯米½碗、紅辣椒1支、荸薺4顆、豆苗1小紮、太白粉1大匙、鹽1小匙、酒½大匙、淡色醬油2大匙。

做法：

1.糯米淘淨，揀去雜質，浸在水中，約4～5小時，濾去水份。

2.荸薺去皮洗淨，切成小粒；豆苗去老葉梗洗淨。

3.豬肉洗淨，去除皮和筋，切成小粒；荸薺粒和入剁碎，加入酒、醬油、太白粉，攪至起黏性，分做成中型肉圓，並沾勻糯米粒。

4.糯米肉圓排列蒸鍋中，約蒸45分鐘後，續燜一下；把糯米肉圓移入瓷盤中，並在肉圓四週加上豆苗，即可遞上餐桌。

備註：

肉圓上所用之糯米，如愛食柔糯的，可用圓糯，或愛食較硬爽的，可採用長糯。

建議：

醣類主要來自糯米，腸胃消化不佳者，不宜多食。

Ingredients

450g minced pork, 75g glutinous rice, 5 water chestnuts.

Seasoning

1 teaspoon salt, 1½ teaspoons rice wine, 2 tablespoons soy sauce, 1 tablespoon cornflour, watercress and chilli for garnish.

Method

1. Wash the rice and soak it in water for 4-5 hours. Drain.
2. Dice the water chestnuts.
3. Marinate the minced pork with the diced water chestnuts. Add salt, rice wine, soy sauce and cornflour. Stir well and shape into balls about 4cm across. Roll the balls in glutinous rice to coat evenly.
4. Steam the rice-coated meatballs for 45 minutes over medium heat. Add more water in if there is not enough in the steamer. Arrange on a plate and garnish with blanched watercress and threads of chilli. Serve.

烤肉捲

BAKED PORK ROLLS

主要營養成份 Major Nutrient Content：

蛋白質 Protein	脂肪 Fat	醣類 Carbohydrate	鈉 Sodium	膽固醇 Cholesterol	總熱量 Total
70 g	148 g	51 g	2960mg	——	1816Cal

材料：

里脊肉450公克、牙籤12支。

①香菇6朵、荸薺8顆、葱4根。

醃料：

太白粉1小匙、糖1大匙、胡椒粉⅛小匙、醬油2大匙、番茄醬2大匙、酒1大匙、醋1大匙、麻油1小匙。

做法：

1. 里脊肉切成12片（半冷凍的肉較易切），用刀背將肉拍出交叉線條，浸於醃料中15分鐘。
2. 香菇浸泡於溫水中15分鐘，瀝乾、去蒂切絲；荸薺、葱切絲，將①料都分成12分，每分用一肉片成捲狀，以牙籤固定。
3. 烤箱先開至200°C，預熱。肉捲放於烤盤，將醃料汁淋上，放入烤箱20分鐘即可取食。

備註：

1. 若為開胃菜可將每一肉捲切成4小捲，以牙籤挿好。
2. 此道菜可預先做好，食時再熱。

Ingredients

450g pork tenderloin.

Stuffing

6 dried mushrooms, 8 water chestnuts, 4 whole scallions.

Marinade

1 teaspoon cornstarch, 1 tablespoon sugar, ⅛ teaspoon pepper, 2 tablespoons soy sauce, 2 tablespoons catchup, 1 tablespoon wine, 1 tablespoon vinegar, 1 teaspoon sesame oil.

---

12 toothpicks.

Method

1. Preheat oven to 200°c. Cut tenderloin crosswise into 12 thin slices. (Partially frozen meat is easier to cut). Pound with a mallet or back of cleaver in a crisscross fashion. Combine with Marinade and let stand for 15 minutes.
2. Soak mushrooms in warm water for 15 minutes. Discard water and stems. Shred mushrooms, water chestnuts and scallions. Roll 1/12th of Stuffing in each slice of pork. Fasten with a toothpick.
3. Arrange rolls in a single layer in a baking dish. Pour excess Marinade over. Bake at 200°C oven for 20 minutes. May be prepared ahead, refrigerated or frozen and re-heated.

西湖牛肉羹

WEST LAKE BEEF SOUP

主要營養成份 Major Nutrient Content：

蛋白質 Protein	脂肪 Fat	醣類 Carbohydrate	鈉 Sodium	膽固醇 Cholesterol	總熱量 Total
49g	13 g	11 g	1000 g	——	357Cal

材料：

里脊牛肉225公克、高湯（可加入適量的鹽）4杯、太白粉水2大匙、蛋白（打勻）2個。

醃料：

太白粉1小匙、糖1小匙、酒1小匙、醬油1大匙。

調味料：

胡椒粉⅛小匙、蔥（切碎）1棵。

做法：

1.逆著牛肉紋理切片，浸醃料中15分鐘。

2.高湯燒開，入牛肉，攪動。湯再滾後，以太白粉水勾芡，再慢慢倒入蛋白，並一面攪動，再滾即可倒入湯碗中，加入胡椒粉和蔥花供食。

Ingredients

225g sirloin or flank, 2 egg whites (beaten), 4 cups broth (seasoned with salt).

Marinade

1 teaspoon cornstarch, 1 teaspoon sugar, 1 teaspoon wine, 1 tablespoon soy sauce.

Seasoning

2 tablespoons cornstarch, ⅛ teaspoon pepper, 1 whole scallion (shredded).

Method

1. Slice beef against grain. Combine with Marinade and let stand for 15 minutes.
2. Bring broth to boil. Add beef and stir. When the broth boils again, thicken with cornstarch mixed with some water. Slowly pour in egg white while stirring. Pour into tureen. Garnish with pepper and scallion.